JEN LUCAS

Sock-Yarn
ACCESSORIES

20 Knitted Designs
with Style and Savvy

Martingale®
Create with Confidence

Dedication

For my sister, Melissa

Sock-Yarn Accessories:
20 Knitted Designs with Style and Savvy
© 2015 by Jen Lucas

Martingale®
19021 120th Ave. NE, Ste. 102
Bothell, WA 98011-9511 USA
ShopMartingale.com

Printed in China
20 19 18 17 16 15   8 7 6 5 4 3 2 1

**Library of Congress Cataloging-in-Publication Data
is available upon request.**

ISBN: 978-1-60468-657-9

MISSION STATEMENT

Dedicated to providing quality products and service to inspire creativity.

CREDITS

PUBLISHER AND CHIEF VISIONARY OFFICER
Jennifer Erbe Keltner

EDITORIAL DIRECTOR
Karen Costello Soltys

DESIGN DIRECTOR
Paula Schlosser

MANAGING EDITOR
Tina Cook

PHOTOGRAPHER
Brent Kane

ACQUISITIONS EDITOR
Karen M. Burns

PRODUCTION MANAGER
Regina Girard

TECHNICAL EDITOR
Amy Polcyn

COVER AND
INTERIOR DESIGNER
Adrienne Smitke

COPY EDITOR
Tiffany Mottet

ILLUSTRATOR
Kathryn Conway

Contents

Introduction

It's been nearly four years since my first book, *Sock-Yarn Shawls*, arrived in yarn stores and you would think by now my stash of sock yarn would have been depleted. I'm going to be completely honest with you—it hasn't been. The sock-yarn stash has only grown—and so have I. While shawls still remain my favorite thing to knit, I've found myself wanting more. I want beautiful accessories that compliment my shawls in cold weather. I want a matching hat and shawl for once. And I want to try to keep that sock-yarn stash under control!

This book aims to help you dive into your own stash and find the perfect yarn to match to your perfect accessory. You will find projects that use two colors, some that use variegated yarn, and even projects knit with self-striping yarn. Be sure to look for the "Make It Your Own!" tip boxes in many of the patterns. These boxes include tips and tricks on how to easily adapt the pattern to get the look you want.

There are 20 projects in this book, so you are sure to find the perfect project for you. The book starts with 12 individual patterns, which include scarves, cowls, mitts, and more. The last eight patterns are organized into four matching sets—there you will find a Fair Isle mitten and hat set as well as sets including socks and shawls.

~ *Jen*

Choosing the Right Yarn

Just as in *Sock-Yarn Shawls* and *Sock-Yarn Shawls II*, I think it's important that we talk about yarn choice. There are many factors to take into consideration when picking out the right sock yarn for your project. Yardage is probably the most important consideration. Lots of sock yarn is hand dyed, so it may be impossible to get another matching skein if you run out. So, just like with any project, make sure you check those yarn labels.

Color is also something to think about when picking yarn for your accessories. Multicolored yarn is beautiful, but sometimes, with a large, complicated stitch pattern, the yarn and stitches fight each other rather than working together to form a beautiful finished piece. I've designed a few projects in this book that will work great for your multicolored yarn. Paragon (page 18) is a perfect scarf for those wildly variegated yarns. The slipped stitches in the pattern help break up the color changes and make a beautiful finished piece. Run Around (page 35) is great for a self-striping yarn. The chevron stitch pattern and afterthought thumb make these mittens perfect for showing off those stripes!

For larger projects that use one color of yarn, you'll want to consider alternating skeins of yarn for the duration of the project, especially if you are using a hand-dyed yarn. For example, the Dundee scarf (page 6) uses a beautiful hand-dyed yarn. But even when yarn skeins are dyed at the same time, they don't always match perfectly. To ensure your project looks one color throughout, switch skeins every two rows. Rather than switching skeins when you run out (causing a noticeable color difference), this method allows the slight differences in skeins to blend together subtly. In "Special Techniques" (page 75), I discuss how to alternate two balls of yarn in your project, whether using one color or two.

≫ **A NOTE ABOUT GAUGE**

All gauges listed in this book are based off a washed, blocked swatch. Take time to check your gauge so you don't run out of yarn!

Finally, fiber content is a very important consideration for choosing the right yarn. Most sock yarns contain at least some wool. My go-to yarns for accessory projects are ones that contain superwash merino. These items are going on someone's head, neck, hands, etc., and for many people, wool yarns that aren't superwash can be a little itchy, especially in those sensitive areas. But what if the recipient is allergic to wool or other animal fibers? Fortunately there are lots of sock yarns out there that don't contain any animal fibers at all. I'd avoid yarn that's 100% cotton because it can be hard to block and doesn't hold its shape well over time. But you can find yarn blends that contain bamboo, Tencel, nylon, silk, and more.

So let's dive into that yarn stash and get knitting!

Dundee

A great beginner scarf pattern, Dundee uses only knits and purls and can be easily adjusted to the size you want.

Designed by author and knit by Jennifer Sinnott

SKILL LEVEL: Beginner ●○○○

FINISHED MEASUREMENTS: 8" x 80"

Materials

2 skeins of Glenhaven Cashmerino Fingering from Three Irish Girls (80% merino, 10% cashmere, 10% nylon; 100 g; 370 yds) in color Padraig (**1**)

US size 5 (3.75 mm) knitting needles, or size needed to obtain gauge

1 stitch marker

Tapestry needle

Blocking wires and/or blocking pins

Gauge

24 sts and 28 rows = 4" in chart patt

Pattern Notes

Chart is on page 8. If you prefer to follow written instructions for the charted material, see "Written Instructions for Chart" on page 8.

If using a hand-dyed yarn, alternate skeins every two rows. See page 77 for more information.

Since this scarf is reversible, once you have completed the first few rows of the scarf, use a stitch marker to mark the right side of the work so you won't lose your place.

» *The textured stitch pattern makes this a great accessory for both men and women.*

Instructions

CO 49 sts. Knit 1 row (WS). Work chart until scarf measures 72" from CO edge. Knit 1 row.

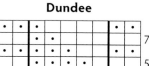

MAKE IT YOUR OWN!

You can adjust the length and width of the scarf very easily. Just add stitches in multiples of 5 (i.e., add 5, 10, 15, etc.) to make the scarf wider. To adjust the length, knit to the desired length, ending with row 8 of the chart, before knitting the final row. Remember, changing the size will affect the amount of yarn required!

Finishing

BO loosely knitwise (page 75). Block scarf to finished measurements given at beg of patt. With tapestry needle, weave in ends.

Written Instructions for Chart

If you prefer to follow row-by-row written instructions rather than a chart, use the instructions below.

Row 1 (RS): K2, *P1, K4; rep from * to last 2 sts, K2.

Row 2 (WS): K2, *P3, K2; rep from * to last 2 sts, K2.

Row 3: K2, *P3, K2; rep from * to last 2 sts, K2.

Row 4: K2, *P1, K4; rep from * to last 2 sts, K2.

Row 5: K2, *K1, P4; rep from * to last 2 sts, K2.

Row 6: K2, *K3, P2; rep from * to last 2 sts, K2.

Row 7: K2, *K3, P2; rep from * to last 2 sts, K2.

Row 8: K2, *K1, P4; rep from * to last 2 sts, K2.

Rep rows 1–8 for patt.

Dundee

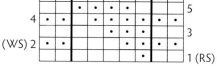

Repeat = 5 sts

Legend

☐ K on RS, P on WS

• P on RS, K on WS

Solitude

SKILL LEVEL: Intermediate ● ● ● ○
SIZES: Adult Small (Adult Large)
FINISHED CIRCUMFERENCE: 18¾ (20½)", fits up to 21 (24)"
FINISHED HEIGHT: 9½ (10)"

Materials

1 skein of Kashmir from Fiber Optic Yarns (80% superwash merino, 10% cashmere, 10% nylon; 114 g; 420 yds) in color Catamaran
US size 2 (2.75 mm) circular needle, 16" cable, and set of double-pointed needles, or size needed to obtain gauge
1 stitch marker
Tapestry needle

Gauge

28 sts and 40 rows = 4" in chart patt

Pattern Notes

Round 5 of the chart ends with a yarn over. Take care not to drop it when starting the next round.

Chart is on page 11. If you prefer to follow written instructions for the charted material, see "Written Instructions for Chart" on page 11.

Instructions

With circular needle, CO 132 (144) sts. PM and join rnd, being careful not to twist.

Rib rnd: *K1, P2; rep from * to end.

Work rib rnd for another 17 (23) rnds. Work rnds 1–12 of chart 6 times total. Work rnds 1–4 of chart once more. Dec as follows, switching to dpns when stitches no longer fit comfortably on 16" circular needle:

Rnd 1: *K5, CDD, K4; rep from * to end—110 (120) sts.

Rnds 2, 4, 6, 8, and 10: Knit.

An interesting lace pattern combined with garter stitch make this slightly slouchy hat one that you'll want to knit again and again!

Designed by author and knit by Gail Nebl

≫ *The lace stitch pattern flows perfectly into the crown decreases.*

Rnd 3: *K4, CDD, K3; rep from * to end—88 (96) sts.

Rnd 5: *K3, CDD, K2; rep from * to end—66 (72) sts.

Rnd 7: *K2, CDD, K1; rep from * to end—44 (48) sts.

Rnd 9: *K1, CDD; rep from * to 3 sts from end of rnd, K1, remove marker, CDD, PM to mark new start of rnd—22 (24) sts.

Rnd 11: K2tog around—11 (12) sts.

Finishing

Cut yarn, leaving an 8" tail. Thread yarn onto tapestry needle and thread through rem sts. Gather sts and tie off. Weave in ends.

Written Instructions for Chart

If you prefer to follow row-by-row written instructions rather than a chart, use the instructions below.

Rnd 1: Purl.

Rnd 2: Knit.

Rnd 3: Purl.

Rnd 4: Knit.

Rnd 5: *K1, YO, K4, CDD, K4, YO; rep from * to end.

Rnd 6: *K2, YO, K3, CDD, K3, YO, K1; rep from * to end.

Rnd 7: *K3, YO, K2, CDD, K2, YO, K2; rep from * to end.

Rnd 8: *K4, YO, K1, CDD, K1, YO, K3; rep from * to end.

Rnd 9: *K5, YO, CDD, YO, K4; rep from * to end.

Rnds 10-12: Knit.

Rep rnds 1-12 for patt.

Solitude

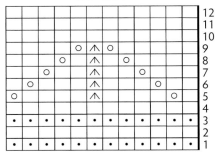

Repeat = 12 sts

Legend

☐ K

• P

◯ YO

⋀ CDD

Adorn

Simple lace and stockinette stitch are the stars of this project. With extra increases added along the top edge, this triangle shawl will stay put on your shoulders, wrapping you like a warm hug.

Designed by author and knit by Melissa Rusk

SKILL LEVEL: Easy ● ● ○ ○
FINISHED MEASUREMENTS: 56" x 18"

Materials

1 skein of Artisan Sock from Hazel Knits (90% superwash merino, 10% nylon; 100 g; 400 yds) in color Sharkskin
US size 5 (3.75 mm) circular needle, 24" cable or longer, or size needed to obtain gauge
2 stitch markers
Tapestry needle
Blocking wires and/or blocking pins

Gauge

18 sts and 32 rows = 4" in St st

Pattern Notes

Chart is on page 15. If you prefer to follow written instructions for the charted material, see "Written Instructions for Chart" on page 14.

Instructions

Work garter tab CO (page 75) as follows: CO 2 sts. Knit 18 rows. Turn work 90° and PU 9 sts along the edge. Turn work 90° and PU 2 sts from CO edge—13 sts total.

SET-UP ROWS

Row 1 (RS): K2, YO, K4, YO, PM, K1, PM, YO, K4, YO, K2—17 sts.

Row 2 (WS): K3, YO, purl to last 3 sts (slipping markers along the way), YO, K3—19 sts.

Work chart 2 times—67 sts.

STOCKINETTE SECTION

Row 1 (RS): K2, YO, knit to marker, YO, SM, K1, SM, YO, knit to last 2 sts, YO, K2—71 sts.

Row 2 (WS): K3, YO, purl to last 3 sts (slipping markers along the way), YO, K3—73 sts.

Rep rows 1 and 2 another 3 times—91 sts.

Work chart 2 times—139 sts.

Work rows 1 and 2 of stockinette section 4 times—163 sts.

Work chart 6 times—307 sts.

STITCH COUNTS	
Following set-up rows	19 sts
Chart	43 sts
Chart	67 sts
Stockinette section	91 sts
Chart	115 sts
Chart	139 sts
Stockinette section	163 sts
Chart	187 sts
Chart	211 sts
Chart	235 sts
Chart	259 sts
Chart	283 sts
Chart	307 sts

 MAKE IT YOUR OWN!

With a second skein of yarn, you can add as many repeats of the chart as you like. You can also switch it up and alternate the chart and stockinette sections to add interest to your shawl. Just be sure to work the full eight rows of the stockinette section or chart before switching!

Finishing

BO loosely knitwise (page 75) on RS. Block shawl to finished measurements given at beg of patt. With tapestry needle, weave in ends.

Written Instructions for Chart

If you prefer to follow row-by-row written instructions rather than a chart, use the instructions below.

Row 1 (RS): K2, YO, K2, *YO, K1, YO, sk2p; rep from * to 1 st before marker, K1, YO, SM, K1, SM, YO, K1, **sk2p, YO, K1, YO; rep from ** to last 4 sts, K2, YO, K2.

Row 2 and all even-numbered rows (WS): K3, YO, purl to last 3 sts, YO, K3.

Row 3: K2, YO, K4, *sk2p, YO, K1, YO; rep from * to 2 sts before marker, K2, YO, SM, K1, SM, YO, K2, **YO, K1, YO, sk2p; rep from ** to last 6 sts, K4, YO, K2.

Row 5: (K2, YO) twice, K1, YO, sk2p, *YO, K1, YO, sk2p; rep from * to 3 sts before marker, K3, YO, SM, K1, SM, YO, K3, **sk2p, YO, K1, YO; rep from ** to last 8 sts, sk2p, YO, K1, (YO, K2) twice.

Row 7: K2, YO, K4, *sk2p, YO, K1, YO; rep from * to 4 sts before marker, K4, YO, SM, K1, SM, YO, K4, **YO, K1, YO, sk2p; rep from ** to last 6 sts, K4, YO, K2.

Row 8: K3, YO, purl to last 3 sts, YO, K3.

Rep rows 1–8 for patt.

≫ *The small lace motif makes this pattern a great choice for multicolored yarn.*

Adorn

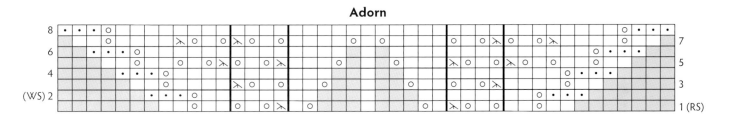

Repeat = 4 sts   Repeat = 4 sts

Legend

☐ K on RS, P on WS   ⊙ YO

• P on RS, K on WS   ⋏ Sk2p

☐ No stitch

Filament

Materials

Staccato from Shibui Knits (70% superwash merino, 30% silk; 50 g; 191 yds) **1**
MC 2 skeins in color Field
CC 2 skeins in color Raspberry
US size 5 (3.75 mm) knitting needles, or size needed to obtain gauge
Tapestry needle
Blocking wires and/or blocking pins

Gauge

20 sts and 32 rows = 4" in patt

Instructions

CO 36 sts.

Row 1 (RS): With MC, *K4, P4; rep from * to last 4 sts, K4.

Row 2 (WS): Rep row 1.

Row 3: With CC, *K4, P4; rep from * to last 4 sts, K4.

Row 4: Rep row 3.

Rep rows 1–4 until scarf measures 70" from CO edge, ending with row 2.

Finishing

With MC, BO loosely knitwise (page 75). Block scarf to finished measurements given at beg of patt. With tapestry needle, weave in ends.

> **MAKE IT YOUR OWN!**
>
> *To change the width of your scarf, add or subtract a multiple of 8 (i.e., add 8, 16, 24, etc.) stitches to your scarf. Remember, adding width to your project will require more yarn. Want a different look for your scarf? Try combining one multicolored yarn with a solid-color yarn and see what kind of interesting scarf emerges!*

With every row worked the same way, this makes for another great beginner scarf pattern. Alternating two colors of yarn every other row adds visual interest to this simple project.

Designed and knit by author

Paragon

Next time you're yarn shopping and are stopped in your tracks by a wildly variegated sock yarn, you'll have the perfect pattern for it! This scarf pattern features slipped stitches, which help prevent color from pooling in your project.

Designed by author and knit by Jenni Lesniak

SKILL LEVEL: Intermediate ● ● ● ○

FINISHED MEASUREMENTS: 6" x 62"

Materials

2 skeins of Socks that Rock Lightweight from Blue Moon Fiber Arts (100% superwash merino; 146 g; 405 yds) in color Electric Kool-Aid Acid Test 🧶**1**

US size 5 (3.75 mm) knitting needles, or size needed to obtain gauge

Tapestry needle

Blocking wires and/or blocking pins

Gauge

24 sts and 32 rows = 4" in St st

Pattern Notes

If using a hand-dyed yarn, alternate skeins every two rows. See page 77 for more information.

Instructions

CO 35 sts. Knit 1 row.

Row 1 (RS): Knit.

Row 2 and all even-numbered rows (WS): K2, purl to last 2 sts, K2.

Row 3: K2, *K1, sl 5 wyif; rep from * to last 3 sts, K3.

Row 5: K5, *insert RH needle under loose strand in front 2 rows below and knit it with next st on LH needle, K5; rep from * to end.

Row 7: K2, sl 3 wyif, K1, *sl 5 wyif, K1; rep from * to last 5 sts, sl 3 wyif, K2.

Row 9: K2, *insert RH needle under loose strand in front 2 rows below and knit it with next st on LH needle, K5; rep from * to last 3 sts, insert RH needle under loose strand in front 2 rows below and knit it with next st on LH needle, K2.

❯ *The slipped stitches in this scarf create an interesting texture and help show off your beautifully variegated sock yarn.*

Row 11: Rep row 3.

Row 13: Rep row 5.

Row 15: Knit.

Row 17: K3, *P1, sl 1 wyif; rep from * to last 4 sts, P1, K3.

Row 18: K2, P1, *sl 1 wyib, K1; rep from * to last 4 sts, sl 1 wyib, P1, K2.

Rep rows 1–18 until scarf measures 54" from CO edge. Rep rows 1–15 once more. Knit 1 row on WS.

❯❯ **MAKE IT YOUR OWN!**

You can adjust the length and width of the scarf very easily. Just add stitches in multiples of 6 (i.e., add 6, 12, 18, etc.) to make the scarf wider. To adjust the length, knit to the desired length, ending with row 15, before knitting the final row. Remember, changing the size will affect the amount of yarn required!

Finishing

BO loosely knitwise (page 75). Block scarf to finished measurements given at beg of patt. With tapestry needle, weave in ends.

Fergus

SKILL LEVEL: Intermediate ● ● ● ○
SIZES: Child Medium (Adult Medium, Adult Extra-Large)
FINISHED FOOT CIRCUMFERENCE: Approx 6 (8, 10)"
FINISHED FOOT LENGTH: Approx 8½ (9½, 10½)", or to desired length

Materials

1 (1, 2) skein of Breathless from Shalimar Yarns (75% superwash merino, 15% cashmere, 10% silk; 113 g; 420 yds) in color Copper Pennies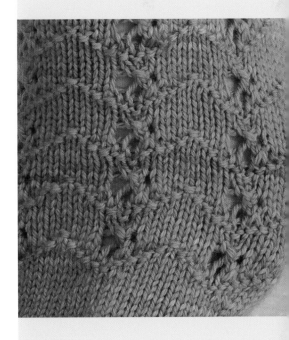
US size 2 (2.75 mm) set of double-pointed needles, or size needed to obtain gauge
1 stitch marker
Tapestry needle

Gauge

34 sts and 40 rows = 4" in St st

Pattern Notes

Charts A, B, and C are on page 24. If you prefer to follow written instructions for the charted material, see "Written Instructions for Charts" on page 24.

With the peaks and valleys created by the purl stitches combined with lace, this stitch pattern is interesting and fun to knit, leaving you ready to knit that second one. No more "single-sock syndrome"!

Designed by author and knit by Jenni Lesniak

Instructions

Make 2.

CO 40 (60, 80) sts. Divide sts evenly on 4 dpns. PM and join rnd, being careful not to twist.

LEG

Ribbing rnd: *P1, K1; rep from * to end.

Rep ribbing rnd another 9 (11, 15) times.

Work rnds 1–8 of chart A once. Work rnds 1–8 of chart B 4 (6, 8) times.

HEEL FLAP

Divide for heel flap as follows: remove marker, K1, heel flap will be worked back and forth in rows over next 19 (29, 39) sts. Rem 21 (31, 41) sts will be held for instep.

Row 1 (RS): Sl 1, K18 (28, 38).

Row 2 (WS): Sl 1, P18 (28, 38).

Rep rows 1 and 2 until heel flap measures 1¾ (2½, 2¾)" or desired length, ending with a WS row.

HEEL TURN

Row 1 (RS): Sl 1, K11 (15, 21), ssk, K1, turn work.

Row 2 (WS): Sl 1, P6 (4, 6), P2tog, P1, turn work.

Row 3: Sl 1, knit to 1 st before gap, ssk to close gap, K1, turn.

Row 4: Sl 1, purl to 1 st before gap, P2tog to close gap, P1, turn.

Rep rows 3 and 4 until all sts have been worked—13 (17, 23) sts.

GUSSET

Set-up rnd: K7 (9, 12), PM to mark new start of rnd. K6 (8, 11) rem heel sts. PU 1 st in each slipped st on side of heel flap. To avoid holes, PU 1 st between heel flap and instep. Work rnd 1 of chart C over next 21 (31, 41) instep sts. PU 1 st between heel flap and instep. PU 1 st in each slipped st along opposite side of heel flap, knit to end of rnd.

Rnd 1: Knit to instep sts, work next rnd of chart C patt over next 21 (31, 41) instep sts, knit to end.

Rnd 2: Knit to 3 sts before instep sts, K2tog, K1, work next rnd of chart C patt over next 21 (31, 41) instep sts, K1, ssk, knit to end.

Rep rnds 1 and 2, working subsequent rnd of chart C patt on each rnd until 40 (60, 80) sts rem.

FOOT

Continue working in patt (working chart C on instep sts and in St st on sole sts), until foot is 1 (1½, 2)" shorter than desired length, ending with rnd 8 of chart C patt.

TOE

Remove marker, K9 (14, 19) sts to end of sole sts. K1 from top-of-foot sts. PM to mark new beg of rnd.

Rnd 1: K1, ssk, knit to last 3 top-of-foot sts, K2tog, K2, ssk, knit to last 3 sts, K2tog, K1— 4 sts dec.

Rnd 2: Knit.

Rep rnds 1 and 2 until 20 (32, 40) sts rem.

Rep rnd 1 only until 12 (16, 16) sts rem.

Finishing

Graft toe using Kitchener st (page 76). Block socks. With tapestry needle, weave in ends.

Written Instructions for Charts

If you prefer to follow row-by-row written instructions rather than a chart, use the instructions below.

CHART A

Rnds 1 and 2: *P1, K9; rep from * to end.

Rnd 3: *P1, K3, YO, sk2p, YO, K3; rep from * to end.

Rnd 4: *K1, P1, K7, P1; rep from * to end.

Rnd 5: *K2, P1, K2, YO, K2tog, K1, P1, K1; rep from * to end.

Rnd 6: *(K3, P1) twice, K2; rep from * to end.

Rnd 7: *K4, P1, K1, P1, K3; rep from * to end.

Rnd 8: *K5, P1, K4; rep from * to end.

CHART B

Rnds 1 and 2: Knit.

Rnd 3: *P1, K3, YO, sk2p, YO, K3; rep from * to end.

Rnd 4: *K1, P1, K7, P1; rep from * to end.

Rnd 5: *K2, P1, K2, YO, K2tog, K1, P1, K1; rep from * to end.

Rnd 6: *(K3, P1) twice, K2; rep from * to end.

Rnd 7: *K4, P1, K1, P1, K3; rep from * to end.

Rnd 8: *K5, P1, K4; rep from * to end.

Rep rnds 1–8 for patt.

CHART C

Note: Chart is worked on instep sts only. Sole sts are worked in St st.

Rnds 1 and 2: Knit.

Rnd 3: *P1, K3, YO, sk2p, YO, K3; rep from * to 1 st before end of instep sts, P1.

Rnd 4: *K1, P1, K7, P1; rep from * to 1 st before end of instep sts, K1.

Rnd 5: *K2, P1, K2, YO, K2tog, K1, P1, K1; rep from * to 1 st before end of instep sts, K1.

Rnd 6: *(K3, P1) twice, K2; rep from * to 1 st before end of instep sts, K1.

Rnd 7: *K4, P1, K1, P1, K3; rep from * to 1 st before end of instep sts, K1.

Rnd 8: *K5, P1, K4; rep from * to 1 st before end of instep sts, K1.

Rep rnds 1–8 for patt.

Fergus Chart A

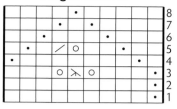

Repeat = 10 sts

Fergus Chart B

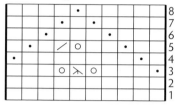

Repeat = 10 sts

Fergus Chart C

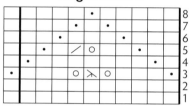

Repeat = 10 sts

Legend

K   Sk2p

P   K2tog

YO

Pleasantville

SKILL LEVEL: Intermediate ● ● ● ○
SIZES: Cowl (Infinity Scarf)
FINISHED CIRCUMFERENCE: 24 (50)", slightly stretched
FINISHED DEPTH: 7½"

Materials

1 (2) skein of Tosh Sock from Madelinetosh (100% superwash merino; 100 g; 395 yds) in color Betty Draper's Blues (1)
US size 3 (3.25 mm) circular needle, 16 (32)" cable, or size needed to obtain gauge
1 stitch marker
Tapestry needle
Blocking wires and/or blocking pins

Gauge

22 sts and 28 rows = 4" in chart patt

Pattern Notes

Pattern is written for cowl with infinity scarf in parentheses. If only one instruction is given, it should be worked for both sizes. Cowl is shown.

Rounds 5 and 7 of chart end with a yarn over. Take care not to drop this stitch when moving on to the next round.

Every 12 rounds, the beginning-of-round stitch marker is moved. Don't forget to move the marker as written in the "Instructions" section while working the chart!

Chart is on page 27. If you prefer to follow written instructions for the charted material, see "Written Instructions for Chart" on page 27.

With instructions for both a small cowl and an infinity scarf, this project is a great use of sock yarn. Combining simple ribbing with lace, this project will look great tucked into your winter coat, no matter which size you knit.

Designed by author and knit by Vickie Zinnel

➤ *The 12-round repeat only contains three rounds where lace stitches are worked—making this project quick to knit and more complicated looking than it actually is!*

Instructions

CO 120 (264) sts. PM and join rnd, being careful not to twist.

Ribbing rnd: K2, *P3, K3; rep from * to last 4 sts, P3, K1.

Rep ribbing rnd for another 5 rnds—6 rnds total.

*Work rnds 1–12 of chart. Remove marker, K3, PM (new start of rnd); rep from * another 3 times—4 chart rep total. Remove marker, K3, PM (new start of rnd). Work ribbing rnd for 10 rnds.

Finishing

BO loosely in patt. Block piece to finished measurements given at beg of patt. With tapestry needle, weave in ends.

Written Instructions for Chart

If you prefer to follow row-by-row written instructions rather than a chart, use the instructions below.

Rnds 1-4: *K2, P3, K1; rep from * to end.

Rnd 5: *K1, YO, ssk, P1, K2tog, YO; rep from * to end.

Rnd 6: *K3, P1, K2; rep from * to end.

Rnd 7: *K1, YO, K1, CDD, K1, YO; rep from * to end.

Rnd 8: Knit.

Rnd 9: *K2, YO, CDD, YO, K1; rep from * to end.

Rnds 10-12: Knit.

Pleasantville

						12
						11
						10
	O	⋀	O			9
						8
O		⋀		O		7
		•				6
O	╱	•	╲	O		5
	•	•	•			4
	•	•	•			3
	•	•	•			2
	•	•	•			1

Repeat = 6 sts

Legend

☐ K	⋀ CDD
• P	╲ Ssk
O YO	╱ K2tog

Larkspur

I've been waiting a long time for just the right project for this lovely lace-stitch pattern. Finally, I've found it—an infinity scarf with a button closure, allowing you to wear the piece a variety of ways. Wear it as a cowl, or unbutton and wear it as a scarf—either way will show off the lace beautifully.

Designed and knit by author

SKILL LEVEL: Intermediate ● ● ● ○
SIZES: Cowl (Infinity Scarf)
FINISHED CIRCUMFERENCE: 24 (70)", slightly stretched
FINISHED DEPTH: 8½"

Materials

2 (3) skeins of Huntington from Valley Yarns (75% fine superwash merino, 25% nylon; 50 g; 218 yds) in color Coffee 🎨1
US size 3 (3.25 mm) circular needle, 16 (32)" cable, or size needed to obtain gauge
1 stitch marker
4 buttons, 1" diameter
Tapestry needle
Blocking wires and/or blocking pins

Gauge

20 sts and 40 rows = 4" in St st

Pattern Notes

Pattern is written for cowl with infinity scarf in parentheses. If only one instruction is given, it should be worked for both sizes. Infinity scarf is shown.

Chart is on page 31. If you prefer to follow written instructions for the charted material, see "Written Instructions for Chart" on page 30.

If using stitch markers to mark each lace pattern repeat, the stitch markers will need to be rearranged on rows 11, 13, and 15 of the chart to accommodate the center double decreases.

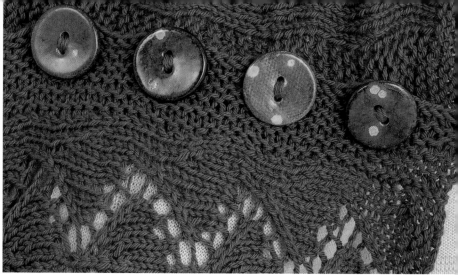

≫ *The larger infinity scarf can easily be wrapped around the neck twice, keeping you warm on a cold winter day.*

Instructions

CO 129 (311) sts.

BEGINNING GARTER BAND

Row 1 (RS): Sl 1 wyib, knit to last 10 sts, PM, knit to end.

Row 2 (WS): Knit to last st, P1.

Row 3: Sl 1 wyib, knit to end.

Rep rows 2 and 3 once more. Rep row 2 once more (3 slipped sts along edge).

BODY OF COWL

Work chart 4 times—32 slipped sts; 35 slipped sts along edge total.

END GARTER BAND

Row 1 (RS): Sl 1 wyib, knit to end.

Row 2 (WS): Knit to last st, P1.

Rep rows 1 and 2 twice more— 3 slipped sts; 38 slipped sts along edge total.

BO loosely knitwise (page 75).

BUTTON BAND

With RS facing, PU 38 slipped sts along edge. Knit 5 rows.

Next row (RS): K5, *K2tog, YO twice, ssk, K4; rep from * to last st, K1.

Next row (WS): *K6, (K1, P1) into double YO; rep from * to last 6 sts, K6.

Knit 4 rows.

BO loosely knitwise (page 75).

> ≫ **MAKE IT YOUR OWN!**
>
> *You can adjust the circumference by adding or subtracting stitches in multiples of 14 (i.e., add 14, 28, 42, etc.). Remember, adjusting the size will affect the amount of yarn required.*

Finishing

Block piece to finished measurements given at beg of patt. With tapestry needle, weave in ends. Sew buttons on button band to match corresponding buttonholes.

Written Instructions for Chart

If you prefer to follow row-by-row written instructions rather than a chart, use the instructions below.

Row 1 (RS): Sl 1 wyib, K7, K2tog, YO, *K1, YO, ssk, K9, K2tog, YO; rep from * to last 21 sts, K1, YO, ssk, K8, SM, K10.

Row 2 and all even-numbered rows (WS): K10, SM, purl to end.

Row 3: Sl 1 wyib, K1, ssk, K3, K2tog, YO, K1, YO, *(K1, YO) twice, ssk, K2, CDD, K2, K2tog, YO, K1, YO; rep from * to last 21 sts, (K1, YO) twice, ssk, K3, K2tog, K2, SM, K10.

Row 5: Sl 1 wyib, K1, ssk, K1, K2tog, YO, K1, YO, K2, *K3, YO, K1, YO, ssk, CDD, K2tog, YO, K1, YO, K2; rep from * to last 21 sts, K3, YO, K1, YO, ssk, K1, K2tog, K2, SM, K10.

Row 7: Sl 1 wyib, K2, K2tog, YO, K5, *K6, YO, CDD, YO, K5; rep from * to last 21 sts, K6, YO, ssk, K3, SM, K10.

Row 9: Sl 1 wyib, K3, YO, ssk, K4, *K5, K2tog, YO, K1, YO, ssk, K4; rep from * to last 21 sts, K5, K2tog, YO, K4, SM, K10.

Row 11: Sl 1 wyib, K3, YO, K1, YO, ssk, K2, *CDD, K2, K2tog, (YO, K1) 3 times, YO, ssk, K2; rep from * to last 22 sts, CDD, K2, K2tog, YO, K1, YO, K4, SM, K10.

Row 13: Sl 1 wyib, K5, YO, K1, YO, ssk, *CDD, K2tog, YO, K1, YO, K5, YO, K1, YO, ssk; rep from * to last 22 sts, CDD, K2tog, YO, K1, YO, K6, SM, K10.

Row 15: Sl 1 wyib, K8, YO, *CDD, YO, K11, YO; rep from * to last 22 sts, CDD, YO, K9, SM, K10.

Row 16: K10, SM, purl to end.

Rep rows 1–16 for patt.

Legend

☐ K on RS, P on WS	╲ Ssk
• P on RS, K on WS	╱ K2tog
○ YO	⋁ Sl 1 wyib
⋀ CDD	☐ Stitch marker

Repeat = 14 sts

Larkspur

Larkspur chart. Rows numbered 1 (RS) through 16 (WS = Row 2).

Rockport

These fingerless mitts feature an easy-to-knit lace pattern that is perfect for mottled yarn. The subtle colors running through the mitts add an interesting dimension.

Designed by author and knit by Jenni Lesniak

SKILL LEVEL: Intermediate ● ● ● ○
FINISHED CIRCUMFERENCE: 6½", fits up to 8½"
FINISHED LENGTH: 7½"

Materials

1 skein of Journey Sock from Unwind Yarn Company (80% superwash merino, 20% nylon; 100 g; 400 yds) in color Abalone ⓵
US size 3 (3.25 mm) set of double-pointed needles, or size needed to obtain gauge
2 stitch markers
Stitch holder or waste yarn
Tapestry needle
Blocking wires and/or blocking pins

Gauge

28 sts and 44 rows = 4" in chart patt

Pattern Notes

Chart is on page 34. If you prefer to follow written instructions for the charted material, see "Written Instructions for Chart" on page 34.

Instructions

Make 2.

CO 44 sts. Divide sts evenly on 4 dpns. PM and join rnd, being careful not to twist.

Ribbing rnd: *P1, K1, P1, (K2, P1) twice, K1, P1; rep from * to end. Rep ribbing rnd for 11 more rnds—12 rnds total.

Working 10-st patt rep 4 times on each rnd, work 4-row chart 10 times—40 rnds total.

THUMB GUSSET

Rnd 1: Work rnd 1 of chart to end of rnd, PM, M1—45 sts.

Rnd 2: Work rnd 2 of chart to marker, SM, K1.

Rnd 3: Work rnd 3 of chart to marker, SM, M1, knit to end of rnd, M1—47 sts.

Rnd 4: Work rnd 4 of chart to marker, SM, knit to end of rnd.

Rnd 5: Work rnd 1 of chart to marker, SM, M1, knit to end of rnd, M1—49 sts.

Rnd 6: Work rnd 2 of chart to marker, SM, knit to end of rnd.

Rep rnds 3–6 twice more—57 sts; 44 sts for hand and 13 sts for thumb.

Rep rnds 3 and 4 once more— 59 sts; 44 sts for hand and 15 sts for thumb.

HAND

Next rnd: Work rnd 1 of chart to marker, remove marker, place next 15 sts on holder or waste yarn.

Work in chart patt for another 3 rnds. Work ribbing rnd for 6 rnds. BO loosely in patt.

THUMB

Carefully transfer 15 held sts from holder to dpns. Place 10 sts on needle #1, 5 sts on needle #2. With needle #3, PU 5 sts in gap where thumb meets hand—20 sts total.

Redistribute sts to 6 sts on needle #1, 8 sts on needle #2, and 6 sts on needle #3.

Rnds 1–3: Knit.

Rnds 4–6: *K1, P1; rep from * to end.

BO thumb sts loosely in patt.

⟫ MAKE IT YOUR OWN!

You can easily add length to these mitts by repeating the chart to the desired length before starting the thumb gusset. Want more length on the hand? Add extra repeats of the chart after transferring stitches to waste yarn for the thumb.

This is another pattern perfect for experimentation with self-striping yarn!

Finishing

Block mitts to finished measurements given at beg of patt. With tapestry needle, weave in ends.

Written Instructions for Chart

If you prefer to follow row-by-row written instructions rather than a chart, use the instructions below.

Rnd 1: *P1, K2, K2tog, YO, K1, YO, ssk, K2, P1; rep from * to end.

Rnd 2: *P1, K1, K2tog, YO, K3, YO, ssk, K1, P1; rep from * to end.

Rnd 3: *P1, K2tog, YO, K5, YO, ssk, P1; rep from * to end.

Rnd 4: *P1, K9, P1; rep from * to end.

Rep rnds 1–4 for patt.

Rockport

Repeat = 11 sts

Legend

☐ K   ＼ Ssk

· P   ／ K2tog

○ YO

Run Around

SKILL LEVEL: Intermediate ● ● ● ○
FINISHED CIRCUMFERENCE: 7½", fits up to 8½"
FINISHED LENGTH: 9½"

Materials

1 skein of SW Stripe from Fresh from the Cauldron (100%
    superwash merino; 100 g; 400 yds) in color Electric Avenue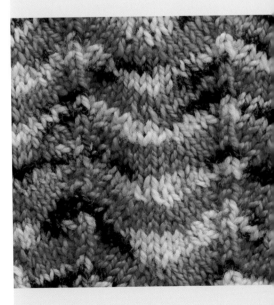
US size 2 (2.75 mm) set of 5 double-pointed needles, or size needed
    to obtain gauge
1 stitch marker
Waste yarn
Tapestry needle
Blocking wires and/or blocking pins

Gauge

32 sts and 36 rows = 4" in hand chart patt in the rnd

Pattern Notes

Charts are on page 39. If you prefer to follow written instructions
for the charted material, see "Written Instructions for Charts" on
page 38.

If you're using a self-striping yarn and want your mittens to match,
make your starting slipknot for the cast on at a color change, making
a note so you remember to start at the same color change on the
second mitten.

The mittens are worked the same except for the thumb placement.
Take care to follow the proper thumb instructions for the second
mitten. No one wants to finish their project with two right-hand
mittens!

Carefully placed increases and decreases create a chevron pattern perfect for all the self-striping sock yarn in your stash. An afterthought thumb is used in order to keep the stripes even throughout the mitten. A fun, quick knit!

Designed and knit by author

Instructions

Make 2.

CO 62 sts. Divide sts on 4 dpns by placing 15 sts on needles 1 and 3 and 16 sts on needles 2 and 4. PM and join rnd, being careful not to twist.

CUFF

Ribbing rnd: *K1 tbl, P1; rep from * to end.

Rep ribbing rnd until mitten measures approx 2½" from CO edge.

HAND

Working chart patt 2 times on each rnd, work hand chart 3 times—24 rnds total.

Working chart patt 2 times on each rnd, work rnds 1–7 of hand chart once more.

RIGHT MITTEN

Next rnd: Knit first 8 sts with waste yarn, slide waste yarn sts back to LH needle and knit them again with the working yarn, knit to end of rnd.

LEFT MITTEN

Next rnd: K23, knit next 8 sts with waste yarn, slide waste yarn sts back to LH needle and knit them again with the working yarn, knit to end of rnd.

For both mittens, working chart patt 2 times on each rnd and starting with rnd 1, work hand chart 3 more times—24 rnds total.

DECREASES

Working chart patt 2 times on each rnd, work decrease chart—17 rnds total; 18 sts rem. Using Kitchener st (page 76), graft top of mitten.

THUMB

Carefully remove waste yarn from thumb sts, placing live sts on 2 dpns. There will be 8 sts on the bottom of the opening and 7 sts on the top. Join yarn at start of needle containing 8 sts. K8, PU 2 sts along gap, K7, PU 2 sts along next gap—19 sts total.

PM and join rnd, being careful not to twist.

Knit all sts each rnd until thumb measures 2½" or ½" shorter than desired length.

Next rnd: K1, (K2tog) 9 times—10 sts.

Next rnd: Knit.

Next rnd: K2tog around—5 sts.

Cut yarn, leaving a 6" tail. Thread yarn onto tapestry needle and thread through remaining sts. Gather sts and tie off.

➤ **MAKE IT YOUR OWN!**

Want to add some length to your mittens? Add extra repeats of the hand chart before working in the waste yarn for the thumb. This pattern would also be great to use up leftover balls of sock yarn. Mix and match your leftovers to create a one-of-a-kind mitten set!

Finishing

Block mittens to finished measurements given at beg of patt. With tapestry needle, weave in ends.

> *Chevrons are created using increases and decreases that don't add holes to your knitting—perfect for keeping your hands warm on a chilly day.*

Written Instructions for Charts

If you prefer to follow row-by-row written instructions rather than a chart, use the instructions below.

HAND CHART

Note: Chart will be worked twice on each round.

Rnd 1: K2tog, K1, M1, K1, *M1, K4, CDD, K4, M1, K1; rep from * once more, M1, K1, ssk.

Rnd 2 and all even-numbered rnds: Knit.

Rnd 3: K2tog, K1, M1, K1, *K1, M1, K3, CDD, K3, M1, K2; rep from * once more, M1, K1, ssk.

Rnd 5: K2tog, K1, M1, K1, *K2, M1, K2, CDD, K2, M1, K3; rep from * once more, M1, K1, ssk.

Rnd 7: K2tog, K1, M1, K1, *K3, M1, K1, CDD, K1, M1, K4; rep from * once more, M1, K1, ssk.

Rnd 8: Knit.

Rep rnds 1–8 for patt.

DECREASE CHART

Note: Chart will be worked twice on each round, once for front of mitten and once for palm.

Rnd 1: K1, ssk, (K1, M1, K4, CDD, K4, M1) twice, K1, K2tog, K1.

Rnds 2, 4, 6, 8, 10, and 12: Knit.

Rnd 3: K1, ssk, K1, M1, K3, CDD, (K3, M1) twice, K3, CDD, K3, M1, K1, K2tog, K1.

Rnd 5: K1, ssk, K1, M1, K2, CDD, K2, M1, K5, M1, K2, CDD, K2, M1, K1, K2tog, K1.

Rnd 7: K1, ssk, K1, M1, K1, CDD, K1, M1, K7, M1, K1, CDD, K1, M1, K1, K2tog, K1.

Rnd 9: K1, ssk, K17, K2tog, K1.

Rnd 11: K1, ssk, K15, K2tog, K1.

Rnd 13: K1, ssk, K13, K2tog, K1.

Rnd 14: K1, ssk, K11, K2tog, K1.

Rnd 15: K1, ssk, K9, K2tog, K1.

Rnd 16: K1, ssk, K7, K2tog, K1.

Rnd 17: K1, ssk, K5, K2tog, K1.

Run Around Hand Chart

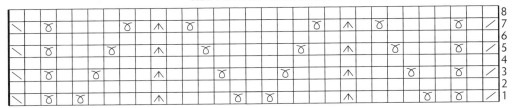

Work repeat twice (mitten front and back).

Run Around Decrease Chart

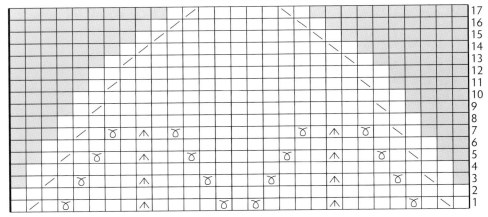

Work repeat twice (mitten front and back).

Legend

☐	K	◿	K2tog
▨	No stitch	୪	M1
◺	Ssk	⋀	CDD

Lake Delton

I named this design after the place my family has been vacationing in Wisconsin for the last two decades. We love spending long weekends at the lake, enjoying family time at the beach. This shawl is perfect for those cool nights sitting lakeside, recounting stories of our childhood.

Designed by author and knit by Elena Duran

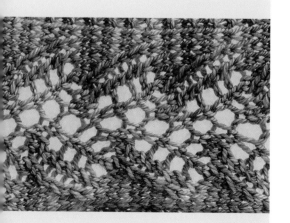

SKILL LEVEL: Experienced ● ● ● ●

FINISHED MEASUREMENTS: 84" x 28"

Materials

2 skeins of Caper Sock from String Theory Hand Dyed Yarn (80% superwash merino, 10% cashmere, 10% nylon; 113 g; 420 yds) in color Jade (1)
US size 5 (3.75 mm) circular needle, 24" cable or longer, or size needed to obtain gauge
Tapestry needle
Blocking wires and/or blocking pins

Gauge

20 sts and 28 rows = 4" in St st

Pattern Notes

Charts are on page 44. If you prefer to follow written instructions for the charted material, see "Written Instructions for Charts" on page 43.

If using a hand-dyed yarn, alternate skeins every two rows. See page 77 for more information.

Instructions

Work garter tab CO (page 75) as follows: CO 2 sts. Knit 24 rows. Turn work 90° and PU 12 sts along the edge. Turn work 90° and PU 2 sts from CO edge—16 sts total.

Set-up row (WS): Knit.

Row 1 (RS): K2, (YO, K1) 6 times, (K1, YO) 6 times, K2—28 sts.

Row 2: K2, purl to last 2 sts, K2.

Row 3: Knit.

Row 4: Rep row 2.

Row 5: K3, (YO, K1) 11 times, (K1, YO) 11 times, K3—50 sts.

Row 6 (WS): Knit.

Work body chart 13 times—258 sts.

Work rows 1–7 of body chart once more—272 sts.

Next row (WS): Knit.

Lace Edging

With RS facing, CO 22 sts using the knitted-on CO.

Row 1 (RS): K21, ssk last border st with first body st on left needle.

Row 2 (WS): Sl 1 wyib, K21.

Rep rows 1 and 2 once more.

Work edge chart 67 times.

Rep rows 1 and 2. Rep row 1 once more.

STITCH COUNTS	
First rep of body chart	66 sts
Second rep of body chart	82 sts
Third rep of body chart	98 sts
Fourth rep of body chart	114 sts
Fifth rep of body chart	130 sts
Sixth rep of body chart	146 sts
Seventh rep of body chart	162 sts
Eighth rep of body chart	178 sts
Ninth rep of body chart	194 sts
Tenth rep of body chart	210 sts
Eleventh rep of body chart	226 sts
Twelfth rep of body chart	242 sts
Thirteenth rep of body chart	258 sts
Final rows 1–7 of body chart	272 sts

≫ *An interesting 8-row lace panel is knitted onto the body of the shawl, adding a lovely, delicate detail to the edge.*

Finishing

BO loosely knitwise (page 75) on WS. Block shawl to finished measurements given at beg of patt. With tapestry needle, weave in ends.

Written Instructions for Charts

If you prefer to follow row-by-row written instructions rather than a chart, use the instructions below.

BODY CHART

Row 1 (RS): K2, YO, K1, K2tog, *YO twice, ssk, K2tog; rep from * to last 5 sts, YO twice, ssk, K1, YO, K2.

Row 2 (WS): K3, YO, *P2, (K1, P1) into double YO; rep from * to last 5 sts, P2, YO, K3.

Row 3: K2, YO, knit to last 2 sts, YO, K2.

Row 4: K3, YO, purl to last 3 sts, YO, K3.

Row 5: K2, YO, K1, YO, *ssk, K2tog, YO twice; rep from * to last 7 sts, ssk, K2tog, YO, K1, YO, K2.

Row 6: K3, YO, P4, (K1, P1) into double YO, P2; rep from * to last 5 sts, P2, YO, K3.

Row 7: Rep row 3.

Row 8: Rep row 4.

Rep rows 1–8 for patt.

EDGE CHART

Row 1 (RS): K4, K2tog twice, (YO, K1) 3 times, YO, ssk twice, K6, ssk last border st with next body st on left needle.

Row 2 and all even-numbered rows (WS): Sl 1 wyib, K2, P17, K2.

Row 3: K3, K2tog twice, YO, K1, YO, K3, YO, K1, YO, ssk twice, K5, ssk last border st with next body st on left needle.

Row 5: K6, K2tog twice, (YO, K1) 3 times, YO, ssk twice, K4, ssk last border st with next body st on left needle.

Row 7: K5, K2tog twice, YO, K1, YO, K3, YO, K1, YO, ssk twice, K3, ssk last border st with next body st on left needle.

Row 8: Sl 1 wyib, K2, P17, K2.

Rep rows 1–8 for patt.

Lake Delton Body Chart

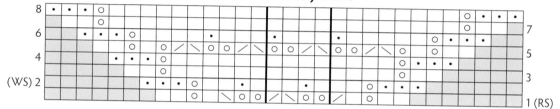

Repeat = 4 sts

Legend

☐ K on RS, P on WS	⊡ YO
⊡ P on RS, K on WS	⧄ K2tog
▨ No stitch	⧅ Ssk

Lake Delton Edge Chart

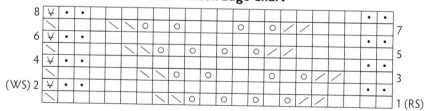

Work final ssk on RS rows as follows:
ssk last border st with next body st on left needle.

Legend

☐ K on RS, P on WS	⧅ Ssk
⊡ P on RS, K on WS	⊡ YO
⧄ K2tog	¥ Sl 1 wyib on WS

Off to Market

SKILL LEVEL: Experienced ● ● ● ●
FINISHED MEASUREMENTS: 11" x 11"

Materials

2 balls of Sox from Berroco (75% superwash wool, 25% nylon; 100 g; 400 yds) in color 1410
US size 3 (3.25 mm) circular needle, 16" cable, and set of double-pointed needles, or size needed to obtain gauge
5 stitch markers
Tapestry needle
Blocking wires and/or blocking pins

Gauge

20 sts and 28 rows = 4" in St st with yarn held doubled

Pattern Notes

Yarn is held doubled for the body of the bag. If using a self-striping yarn as shown, match up the stripes before starting to knit—this will create even stripes for your project.

Several stitch markers are used in the construction of the bag. You may wish to use a different color to mark the beginning of the round, to help you keep track of your work.

This small satchel is great for a quick trip to the farmers' market or running to knit group with a small project in tow. The bag is worked with the yarn held doubled, adding durability. It's ready to carry whatever you decide to pack!

Designed and knit by author

≫ *Weaving I-cord through the holes along the sides allows you to adjust the straps to the desired length.*

Instructions

The bag is worked from the bottom up, beginning at the center of the bag bottom.

BAG BOTTOM

With dpns and yarn held doubled, CO 6 sts. Divide sts evenly on 3 dpns. PM and join rnd, being careful not to twist.

Note: Switch to 16" circular needle when stitches no longer fit comfortably on dpns.

Rnd 1: K1f&b around—12 sts.

Rnd 2 and all even-numbered rnds: Knit.

Rnd 3: *K1f&b, K1; rep from * to end—18 sts.

Rnd 5: *K1f&b, K2; rep from * to end—24 sts.

Rnd 7: *K1f&b, K3; rep from * to end—30 sts.

Rnd 9: *K1f&b, K4; rep from * to end—36 sts.

Rnd 11: *K1f&b, K5; rep from * to end—42 sts.

Rnd 13: *K1f&b, K6; rep from * to end—48 sts.

Rnd 15: *K1f&b, K7; rep from * to end—54 sts.

Rnd 17: *K1f&b, K8; rep from * to end—60 sts.

Rnd 19: *K1f&b, K9; rep from * to end—66 sts.

Rnd 21: *K1f&b, K10; rep from * to end—72 sts.

Rnd 23: *K1f&b, K11; rep from * to end—78 sts.

Rnd 25: *K1f&b, K12; rep from * to end—84 sts.

Rnd 27: *K1f&b, K13; rep from * to end—90 sts.

Rnd 29: *K1f&b, K14; rep from * to end—96 sts.

Rnd 31: *K1f&b, K15; rep from * to end—102 sts.

Rnd 33: *K1f&b, K16; rep from * to end—108 sts.

Rnd 35: *K1f&b, K17; rep from * to end—114 sts.

Rnd 37: *K1f&b, K18; rep from * to end—120 sts.

Rnd 38: Knit.

BAG BODY

Set-up rnd 1: Purl all sts.

Set-up rnd 2: K22, PM, (P2, K5) twice, P2, PM, K44, PM, (P2, K5) twice, P2, PM, K22.

Rnd 1: *Knit to marker, SM, P2, K1, K2tog, YO twice, ssk, P2, K2tog, YO twice, ssk, K1, P2, SM; rep from * once more, knit to end.

Rnd 2: *Knit to marker, SM, P2, K2, (K1, P1) into double YO, K1, P2, K1, (K1, P1) into double YO, K2, P2, SM; rep from * once more, knit to end.

Rnds 3–8: *Knit to marker, SM, (P2, K5) twice, P2, SM; rep from * once more, knit to end.

Rep rnds 1–8 another 4 times. Rep rnds 1–3 once more—6 sets of eyelet holes on each side total.

UPPER EDGE

Rnd 1: Purl, removing 4 markers (keep marker for beg of rnd).

Rnd 2: *K10, K2tog; rep from * to end—110 sts.

Rnd 3: Knit.

Rnd 4: Purl.

BO loosely knitwise (page 75).

I-CORD HANDLES

Make 2.

With dpns and 1 strand of yarn, CO 4 sts. Work in I-cord until cord measures 50".

Final I-cord rnd: K2tog twice, pass one stitch over the other and fasten off.

Finishing

Block bag to finished measurements given at beg of patt. With tapestry needle, weave in ends. Weave I-cord handles into eyelets along sides of bag as follows:

Starting at bottom of bag, insert I-cord into each hole, going from outside to inside of bag. Weave handles corset-style (cross straps on exterior, thread each through one hole, cross on interior and thread out through next set of holes and repeat) up one side of bag. Continue weaving handles on second side of back, starting at top of bag and working in same manner as first side. Adjust length of handles by gently pulling on ends, then flattening sides. Tie I-cord ends into a bow on each side.

Cobblestone

COWL

SKILL LEVEL: Easy ● ● ○ ○

SIZES: Cowl (Infinity Scarf)

FINISHED CIRCUMFERENCE: 22 (44)" slightly stretched

FINISHED DEPTH: 9"

Materials

1 (2) skein of Breathless from Shalimar Yarns (75% superwash merino, 15% cashmere, 10% silk; 113 g; 420 yds) in color Mole (**1**)

US size 4 (3.5 mm) circular needle, 16 (32)" cable, or size needed to obtain gauge

2 stitch markers

Tapestry needle

Blocking wires and/or blocking pins

Gauge

24 sts and 40 rows = 4" in chart patt

Pattern Notes

Pattern is written for cowl with infinity scarf in parentheses. If only one instruction is given, it should be worked for both sizes. Infinity scarf is shown.

Chart is on page 51. If you prefer to follow written instructions for the charted material, see "Written Instructions for Chart" on page 51.

Instructions

CO 66 (132) sts, PM, CO 66 (132 sts)—132 (264) sts total. PM and join rnd, being careful not to twist.

Ribbing rnd: P2, *K2, P4; rep from * to 4 sts from end of rnd, K2, P2. Rep ribbing rnd for 11 more rnds—12 rnds total.

A simple stitch pattern has the volume turned up when worked in the mirror image on both a comfy cowl and coordinating fingerless mitts.

Designed by author and knit by Jenni Lesniak

> ➢ *By mirroring the stitch pattern on the second half of the cowl, an interesting V pattern forms at the center of the cowl.*

Work rep A 11 (22) times on each rnd, then work rep 11 (22) times to end of rnd. (**Note:** Chart will be worked for 72 rnds total.)

Work ribbing rnd for 12 rnds.

➢➢ **MAKE IT YOUR OWN!**

You can adjust the circumference by adding or subtracting stitches in multiples of 12 (i.e. add 12, 24, 36, etc.). You will need to work the same number of repeats on each half of the cowl. Remember, adjusting the size will affect the amount of yarn required.

Finishing

BO loosely in patt. Block cowl to finished measurements given at beg of patt. With tapestry needle, weave in ends.

Written Instructions for Chart

If you prefer to follow row-by-row written instructions rather than a chart, use the instructions below.

Rnds 1–4: *K4, P2; rep from * 11 (22) times to marker, SM, *P2, K4; rep from * 11 (22) times to end.

Rnds 5–8: *K2, P2, K2; rep from * 11 (22) times to marker, SM, *K2, P2, K2; rep from * 11 (22) times to end.

Rnds 9–12: *P2, K4; rep from * 11 (22) times to marker, SM, *K4, P2; rep from * 11 (22) times to end.

Rep rnds 1–12 for patt.

Cobblestone Cowl

•	•								•	•	12
•	•								•	•	11
•	•								•	•	10
•	•								•	•	9
		•	•				•	•			8
		•	•				•	•			7
		•	•				•	•			6
		•	•				•	•			5
				•	•	•	•				4
				•	•	•	•				3
				•	•	•	•				2
				•	•	•	•				1

Repeat B = 6 sts   Repeat A = 6 sts
Work 11(12) times.   Work 11(12) times.

Legend

☐ K

• P

FINGERLESS MITTS

SKILL LEVEL: Intermediate ● ● ● ○
FINISHED CIRCUMFERENCE: 6½", fits up to 8½"
FINISHED LENGTH: 8½"

Materials

1 skein of Breathless from Shalimar Yarns (75% superwash merino, 15% cashmere, 10% silk; 113 g; 420 yds) in color Mole (**1**)
US size 2 (2.75 mm) set of double-pointed needles, or size needed to obtain gauge
2 stitch markers
Stitch holder or waste yarn
Tapestry needle

Gauge

32 sts and 40 rows = 4" in chart patt in the rnd

Pattern Notes

Charts are on page 53. If you prefer to follow written instructions for the charted material, see "Written Instructions for Charts" on page 53.

Right Mitt

CO 48 sts. Divide sts evenly on 4 dpns. PM and join rnd, being careful not to twist.

Ribbing rnd: P2, *K2, P4; rep from * to 4 sts from end of rnd, K2, P2.

Rep ribbing rnd 11 more times—12 rnds total.

Working right mitt chart, work 6-st rep 8 times on each rnd, work 12-rnd patt 4 times—48 rnds total.

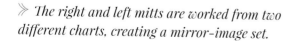

≫ *The right and left mitts are worked from two different charts, creating a mirror-image set.*

THUMB GUSSET

Rnd 1: Work rnd 1 of right mitt chart to end, PM, M1—49 sts.

Rnd 2: Work rnd 2 of right mitt chart to marker, SM, K1.

Rnd 3: Work next rnd of right mitt chart to marker, SM, M1, knit to end, M1—51 sts.

Rnd 4: Work next rnd of right mitt chart to marker, SM, knit to end.

Continue working in patt for right mitt chart on subsequent rows (starting with rnd 5); rep rnds 3 and 4 another 6 times—63 sts; 48 sts for hand and 15 sts for thumb.

HAND

Next rnd: Work next rnd of right mitt chart to marker, remove marker, place 15 sts on holder or waste yarn.

Work in right mitt chart patt for another 7 rnds. Work ribbing rnd for 6 rnds. BO loosely in patt.

THUMB

Carefully transfer 15 held sts from holder to dpns. Place 10 sts on needle #1 and 5 sts on needle #2. With needle #3, PU 5 sts in gap where thumb meets hand—20 sts total.

Redistribute sts to 6 sts on needle #1, 8 sts on needle #2, and 6 sts on needle #3.

Rnds 1–3: Knit.

Rnds 4–6: *K1, P1; rep from * to end.

BO loosely in patt.

Left Mitt

Using left mitt chart, work left mitt same as right mitt.

Finishing

Block mitts to finished measurements given at beg of patt. With tapestry needle, weave in ends.

Written Instructions for Charts

If you prefer to follow row-by-row written instructions rather than a chart, use the instructions below.

RIGHT MITT

Rnds 1–4: *K4, P2; rep from * to end.

Rnds 5–8: *K2, P2, K2; rep from * to end.

Rnds 9–12: *P2, K4; rep from * to end.

Rep rnds 1–12 for patt.

LEFT MITT

Rnds 1–4: *P2, K4; rep from * to end.

Rnds 5–8: *K2, P2, K2; rep from * to end.

Rnds 9–12: *K4, P2; rep from * to end.

Rep rnds 1–12 for patt.

Cobblestone Right Mitt

Cobblestone Left Mitt

Legend

☐ K

⊡ P

Forest Walk

Beautiful lace motifs fall all over this shawl and hat set. The stitch pattern from the hat is worked as a center panel on the shawl, and a wool-and-silk-blend yarn is used to keep both items light and airy.

Designed by author and
knit by Cathy Rusk

SHAWL

SKILL LEVEL: Experienced ● ● ● ●
FINISHED MEASUREMENTS: 66" x 13"

Materials

1 skein of Silky from JulieSpins (50% silk, 50% superwash merino; 100 g; 435 yds) in color Lilac (**1**)
US size 5 (3.75 mm) circular needle, 24" cable or longer, or size needed to obtain gauge
2 stitch markers
Tapestry needle
Blocking wires and/or blocking pins

Gauge

20 sts and 36 rows = 4" in St st

Pattern Notes

Charts are on page 58. If you prefer to follow written instructions for the charted material, see "Written Instructions for Charts" on page 56.

Instructions

CO 49 sts.

Set-up row (WS): K2, (P15, PM) twice, P15, K2.

Work chart A 6 times—289 sts.

Work chart B once—315 sts.

STITCH COUNTS	
First rep of chart A	89 sts
Second rep of chart A	129 sts
Third rep of chart A	169 sts
Fourth rep of chart A	209 sts
Fifth rep of chart A	249 sts
Sixth rep of chart A	289 sts
Chart B	315 sts

➢ **MAKE IT YOUR OWN!**
With a second skein of yarn, you can add as many repeats of chart A as you like before working chart B.

Finishing

BO loosely purlwise (page 76) on WS. Block shawl to finished measurements given at beg of patt. With tapestry needle, weave in ends.

Written Instructions for Charts

If you prefer to follow row-by-row written instructions rather than a chart, use the instructions below.

CHART A

Row 1 (RS): K2, YO, K1, *K3, YO, sk2p, YO, K4; rep from * to 4 sts before marker, K2, YO, K2tog, SM, P1, K10, K2tog, YO, K1, P1, SM, ssk, YO, K2, **K4, YO, sk2p, YO, K3; rep from ** to last 3 sts, K1, YO, K2.

Row 2 (WS): K3, YO, purl to marker, SM, K1, YO, P2, P2tog, P9, K1, SM, purl to last 3 sts, YO, K3.

Row 3: K2, YO, K3, *K2, K2tog, YO, K1, YO, ssk, K3; rep from * to 4 sts before marker, K2, YO, K2tog, SM, P1, K8, K2tog, K1, YO, K2, P1, SM, ssk, YO, K2, **K3, K2tog, YO, K1, YO, ssk, K2; rep from ** to last 5 sts, K3, YO, K2.

Row 4: K3, YO, purl to marker, SM, K1, P1, YO, P3, P2tog, P7, K1, SM, purl to last 3 sts, YO, K3.

Row 5: K2, YO, K5, *K1, K2tog, YO, K3, YO, ssk, K2; rep from * to 4 sts before marker, K2, YO, K2tog, SM, P1, K6, K2tog, K2, YO, K3, P1, SM, ssk, YO, K2, **K2, K2tog, YO, K3, YO, ssk, K1; rep from ** to last 7 sts, K5, YO, K2.

Row 6: K3, YO, purl to marker, SM, K1, P2, YO, P4, P2tog, P5, K1, SM, purl to last 3 sts, YO, K3.

Row 7: K2, YO, K4, YO, ssk, K1, *K2tog, YO, K5, YO, ssk, K1; rep from * to 4 sts before marker, K2, YO, K2tog, SM, P1, K4, K2tog, K3, YO, K4, P1, SM, ssk, YO, K2, **K1, K2tog, YO, K5, YO, ssk; rep from ** to last 9 sts, K1, K2tog, YO, K4, YO, K2.

Row 8: K3, YO, purl to marker, SM, K1, P3, YO, P5, P2tog, P3, K1, SM, purl to last 3 sts, YO, K3.

Row 9: K2, YO, K1, YO, K2tog, YO, K4, YO, sk2p, *YO, K7, YO, sk2p; rep from * to 3 sts before marker, YO, K1, YO, K2tog, SM, P1, K1, YO, ssk, K10, P1, SM, ssk, YO, K1, YO, **sk2p, YO, K7, YO; rep from ** to last 12 sts, sk2p, YO, K4, YO, ssk, YO, K1, YO, K2.

Row 10: K3, YO, purl to marker, SM, K1, P9, P2tog tbl, P2, YO, K1, SM, purl to last 3 sts, YO, K3.

Row 11: K2, YO, K1, YO, K2tog, YO, K6, K2tog, YO, K1, *YO, ssk, K5, K2tog, YO, K1; rep from * to 4 sts before marker, K2, YO, K2tog, SM, P1, K2, YO, K1, ssk, K8, P1, SM, ssk, YO, K2, **K1, YO, ssk, K5, K2tog, YO; rep from ** to last 14 sts, K1, YO, ssk, K6, YO, ssk, YO, K1, YO, K2.

Row 12: K3, YO, purl to marker, SM, K1, P7, P2tog tbl, P3, YO, P1, K1, SM, purl to last 3 sts, YO, K3.

Row 13: K2, YO, K1, YO, K2tog, YO, K2, *K1, YO, ssk, K3, K2tog, YO, K2; rep from * to 4 sts before marker, K2, YO, K2tog, SM, P1, K3, YO, K2, ssk, K6, P1,

> *With a leafy center panel, this shawl is a great accessory for your favorite outdoor activities on a cool spring day.*

SM, ssk, YO, K2, **K2, YO, ssk, K3, K2tog, YO, K1; rep from ** to last 7 sts, K2, YO, ssk, YO, K1, YO, K2.

Row 14: K3, YO, purl to marker, SM, K1, P5, P2tog tbl, P4, YO, P2, K1, SM, purl to last 3 sts, YO, K3.

Row 15: K2, YO, K1, YO, K2tog, YO, K5, *K2, YO, ssk, K1, K2tog, YO, K3; rep from * to 4 sts before marker, K2, YO, K2tog, SM, P1, K4, YO, K3, ssk, K4, P1, SM, ssk, YO, K2, **K3, YO, ssk, K1, K2tog, YO, K2; rep from ** to last 10 sts, K5, YO, ssk, YO, K1, YO, K2.

Row 16: K3, YO, purl to marker, SM, K1, P3, P2tog tbl, P5, YO, P3, K1, SM, purl to last 3 sts, YO, K3.

Rep rows 1–16 for patt.

CHART B

Row 1 (RS): K2, YO, K1, *K3, YO, sk2p, YO, K4; rep from * to 4 sts before marker, K2, YO, K2tog, SM, P1, K10, K2tog, YO, K1, P1, SM, ssk, YO, K2, **K4, YO, sk2p, YO, K3; rep from ** to last 3 sts, K1, YO, K2.

Row 2 (WS): K3, YO, purl to marker, SM, K1, YO, P2, P2tog, P9, K1, SM, purl to last 3 sts, YO, K3.

Row 3: K2, YO, K3, *K2, K2tog, YO, K1, YO, ssk, K3; rep from * to 4 sts before marker, K2, YO, K2tog, SM, P1, K8, K2tog, K1, YO, K2, P1, SM, ssk, YO, K2, **K3, K2tog, YO, K1, YO, ssk, K2; rep from ** to last 5 sts, K3, YO, K2.

Row 4: K3, YO, purl to marker, SM, K1, P1, YO, P3, P2tog, P7, K1, SM, purl to last 3 sts, YO, K3.

Row 5: K2, YO, K5, *K1, K2tog, YO, K3, YO, ssk, K2; rep from * to 4 sts before marker, K2, YO, K2tog, SM, P1, K6, K2tog, K2, YO, K3, P1, SM, ssk, YO, K2, **K2, K2tog, YO, K3, YO, ssk, K1; rep from ** to last 7 sts, K5, YO, K2.

Row 6: K3, YO, purl to marker, SM, K1, P2, YO, P4, P2tog, P5, K1, SM, purl to last 3 sts, YO, K3.

Row 7: K2, YO, K4, YO, ssk, K1, *K2tog, YO, K1, YO, sk2p, YO, K1, YO, ssk, K1; rep from * to 4 sts before marker, K2, YO, K2tog, SM, P1, K4, K2tog, K3, YO, K4, P1, SM, ssk, YO, K2,

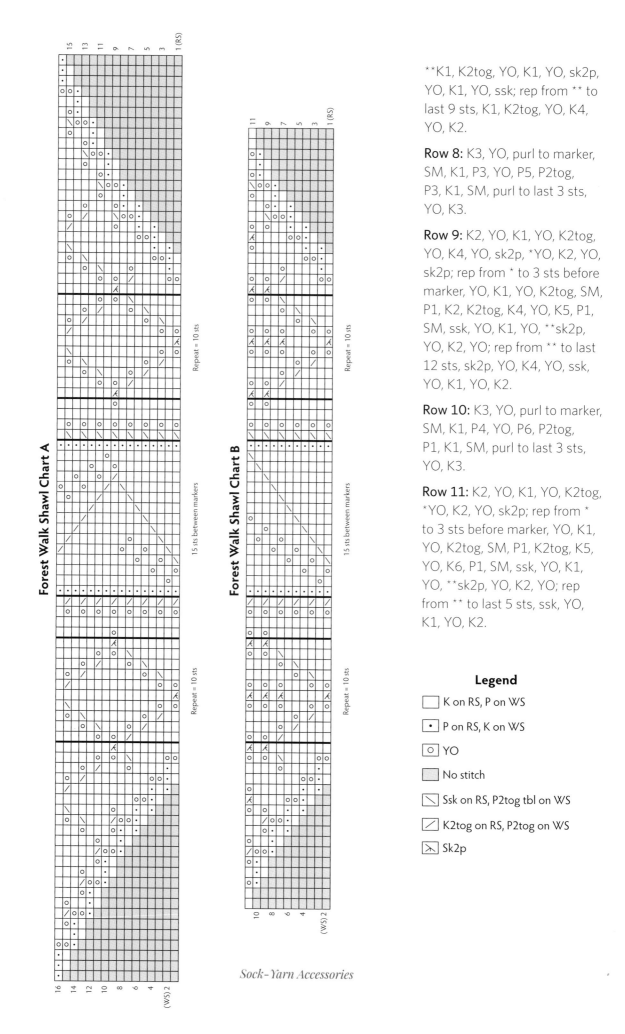

Forest Walk Shawl Chart A

Forest Walk Shawl Chart B

15 sts between markers

Repeat = 10 sts

**K1, K2tog, YO, K1, YO, sk2p, YO, K1, YO, ssk; rep from ** to last 9 sts, K1, K2tog, YO, K4, YO, K2.

Row 8: K3, YO, purl to marker, SM, K1, P3, YO, P5, P2tog, P3, K1, SM, purl to last 3 sts, YO, K3.

Row 9: K2, YO, K1, YO, K2tog, YO, K4, YO, sk2p, *YO, K2, YO, sk2p; rep from * to 3 sts before marker, YO, K1, YO, K2tog, SM, P1, K2, K2tog, K4, YO, K5, P1, SM, ssk, YO, K1, YO, **sk2p, YO, K2, YO; rep from ** to last 12 sts, sk2p, YO, K4, YO, ssk, YO, K1, YO, K2.

Row 10: K3, YO, purl to marker, SM, K1, P4, YO, P6, P2tog, P1, K1, SM, purl to last 3 sts, YO, K3.

Row 11: K2, YO, K1, YO, K2tog, *YO, K2, YO, sk2p; rep from * to 3 sts before marker, YO, K1, YO, K2tog, SM, P1, K2tog, K5, YO, K6, P1, SM, ssk, YO, K1, YO, **sk2p, YO, K2, YO; rep from ** to last 5 sts, ssk, YO, K1, YO, K2.

Legend

☐ K on RS, P on WS

• P on RS, K on WS

⊡ YO

▨ No stitch

╲ Ssk on RS, P2tog tbl on WS

╱ K2tog on RS, P2tog on WS

⅄ Sk2p

HAT

SKILL LEVEL: Intermediate ● ● ● ○
FINISHED CIRCUMFERENCE: 18", fits up to 22"
FINISHED LENGTH: 10"

Materials

1 skein of Silky from JulieSpins (50% silk, 50% superwash merino; 100 g; 435 yds) in color Lilac (1)

US size 6 (4 mm) circular needle, 16" cable, and set of double-pointed needles, or size needed to obtain gauge

US size 3 (3.25 mm) circular needle, 16" cable

1 stitch marker

Tapestry needle

Gauge

20 sts and 28 rows = 4" in chart patt with larger needles in the rnd

Pattern Notes

Chart is on page 61. If you prefer to follow written instructions for the charted material, see "Written Instructions for Chart" on page 61.

Instructions

With smaller circular needle, cast on 119 sts. PM and join rnd, being careful not to twist.

Ribbing rnd: *(P1, K1) 8 times, P1; rep from * to end.

Rep ribbing rnd another 13 times—14 rnds total. Switch to larger circular needle and knit 1 rnd. Working chart 7 times on each rnd of hat, work rnds 1–20 of hat patt 3 times—60 rnds total.

≫ *The decreases form nicely finished leaves at the crown of the hat.*

> ⇗ *This slouchy hat pattern complements the shawl without matching it too precisely.*

SHAPE CROWN

Note: Switch to dpns when stitches no longer fit comfortably on 16" circular needle.

Rnd 1: *P1, K12, K2tog, K1, P1; rep from * to end—112 sts.

Rnd 2: *P1, K10, K2tog, K2, P1; rep from * to end—105 sts.

Rnd 3: *P1, K8, K2tog, K3, P1; rep from * to end—98 sts.

Rnd 4: *P1, K6, K2tog, K4, P1; rep from * to end—91 sts.

Rnd 5: *P1, K4, K2tog, K5, P1; rep from * to end—84 sts.

Rnd 6: *P1, K2, K2tog, K6, P1; rep from * to end—77 sts.

Rnd 7: *P1, K2tog, K7, P1; rep from * to end—70 sts.

Rnd 8: *K2tog, K7, P1; rep from * to end—63 sts.

Rnd 9: *K2tog, K6, P1; rep from * to end—56 sts.

Rnd 10: *K2tog, K5, P1; rep from * to end—49 sts.

Rnd 11: *K2tog, K4, P1; rep from * to end—42 sts.

Rnd 12: *K2tog, K3, P1; rep from * to end—35 sts.

Rnd 13: *K2tog, K2, P1; rep from * to end—28 sts.

Rnd 14: *K2tog, K1, P1; rep from * to end—21 sts.

Rnd 15: *K2tog, P1; rep from * to end—14 sts.

⇗ **MAKE IT YOUR OWN!**

If you want a less slouchy hat, the pattern is easy to alter. Eliminate one repeat of the chart before working the crown decreases.

Finishing

Cut yarn, leaving an 8" tail. Thread yarn onto tapestry needle and thread through remaining sts. Gather sts and tie off. Weave in ends. Block hat to dimensions given at beg of patt.

Written Instructions for Chart

If you prefer to follow row-by-row written instructions rather than a chart, use the instructions below.

Rnd 1: *P1, K12, K2tog, YO, K1, P1; rep from * to end.

Rnd 2: *P1, K11, K2tog, K2, YO, P1; rep from * to end.

Rnd 3: *P1, K10, K2tog, K1, YO, K2, P1; rep from * to end.

Rnd 4: *P1, K9, K2tog, K3, YO, K1, P1; rep from * to end.

Rnd 5: *P1, K8, K2tog, K2, YO, K3, P1; rep from * to end.

Rnd 6: *P1, K7, K2tog, K4, YO, K2, P1; rep from * to end.

Rnd 7: *P1, K6, K2tog, K3, YO, K4, P1; rep from * to end.

Rnd 8: *P1, K5, K2tog, K5, YO, K3, P1; rep from * to end.

Rnd 9: *P1, K4, K2tog, K4, YO, K5, P1; rep from * to end.

Rnd 10: *P1, K3, K2tog, K6, YO, K4, P1; rep from * to end.

Rnd 11: *P1, K1, YO, ssk, K12, P1; rep from * to end.

Rnd 12: *P1, YO, K2, ssk, K11, P1; rep from * to end.

Rnd 13: *P1, K2, YO, K1, ssk, K10, P1; rep from * to end.

Rnd 14: *P1, K1, YO, K3, ssk, K9, P1; rep from * to end.

Rnd 15: *P1, K3, YO, K2, ssk, K8, P1; rep from * to end.

Rnd 16: *P1, K2, YO, K4, ssk, K7, P1; rep from * to end.

Rnd 17: *P1, K4, YO, K3, ssk, K6, P1; rep from * to end.

Rnd 18: *P1, K3, YO, K5, ssk, K5, P1; rep from * to end.

Rnd 19: *P1, K5, YO, K4, ssk, K4, P1; rep from * to end.

Rnd 20: *P1, K4, YO, K6, ssk, K3, P1; rep from * to end.

Forest Walk Hat

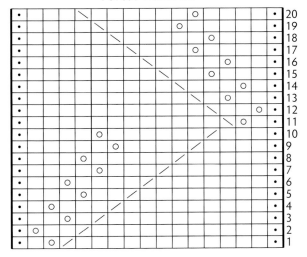

Repeat = 17 sts

Legend

☐ K	◥ Ssk
• P	◢ K2tog
◉ YO	

Crossing Paths

This winter set is sure to challenge knitters who are ready to turn up their sock-yarn knitting a notch. Beautiful solid-colored yarn paired with stranded colorwork makes a great matching accessory set that shows off your knitting skills!

Designed and knit by author

HAT

SKILL LEVEL: Experienced ● ● ● ●
SIZES: Adult Small (Adult Large)
FINISHED CIRCUMFERENCE: 20", fits up to 22" (22", fits up to 24")
FINISHED LENGTH: 9"

Materials

Gloss Fingering from Knit Picks (70% merino, 30% silk; 50 g; 220 yds) **1**
MC 1 skein in color Robot
CC 1 skein in color Kenai
US size 2 (2.75 mm) circular needle, 16" cable, and set of double-pointed needles, or size needed to obtain gauge
1 stitch marker
Tapestry needle

Gauge

30 sts and 32 rows = 4" in chart patt in the rnd

Pattern Notes

Chart is on page 64.

Take care to keep floats on wrong side of work at an even tension.

Pattern is written for Adult Small with Adult Large in parentheses. If only one instruction is given, it should be worked for both sizes. Adult Small is shown.

Instructions

With circular needle and MC, CO 140 (152) sts. PM and join rnd, being careful not to twist.

Ribbing rnd: With MC, *K2, P2; rep from * to end.

Rep ribbing rnd another 15 times—16 rnds total.

> *This stitch pattern would look great in a variety of contrasting colors.*

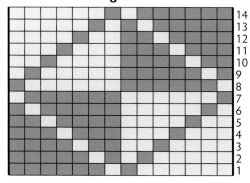

MAKE IT YOUR OWN!

You can easily add length to your hat in two places. Work extra rounds of the ribbing or add extra rows of stockinette stitch before working the crown decreases. If you add length to your hat, remember that you may need extra main-color yarn.

Adult Small only

With MC, knit 3 rnds.

Adult Large only

With MC, knit 1 rnd.

Next rnd: With MC, K2, M1, knit to last 2 sts, M1, K2—154 sts.

Next rnd: With MC, knit.

Both sizes

Work rnds 1–14 of chart 2 times total. Work rnds 1–7 of chart once more. Cut CC. MC will be used for remainder of hat. Knit 2 rnds.

SHAPE CROWN

Dec as follows, switching to dpns when stitches no longer fit comfortably on 16" circular needle.

Rnd 1: *K2tog, K10, ssk; rep from * to end—120 (132) sts.

Rnds 2 and 3: Knit.

Rnd 4: *K2tog, K8, ssk; rep from * to end—100 (110) sts.

Rnds 5 and 6: Knit.

Rnd 7: *K2tog, K6, ssk; rep from * to end—80 (88) sts.

Rnds 8 and 9: Knit.

Rnd 10: *K2tog, K4, ssk; rep from * to end—60 (66) sts.

Rnds 11 and 12: Knit.

Rnd 13: *K2tog, K2, ssk; rep from * to end—40 (44) sts.

Rnd 14: Knit.

Rnd 15: *K2tog, ssk; rep from * to end—20 (22) sts.

Rnd 16: *K2tog; rep from * to end—10 (11) sts.

Finishing

Cut yarn, leaving an 8" tail. Thread yarn onto tapestry needle and thread through remaining sts. Gather sts and tie off. Weave in ends.

Block hat to finished measurements given at beg of patt. With tapestry needle, weave in ends.

Crossing Paths Hat

Repeat = 14 sts

Legend

☐ K with MC

☐ K with CC

MITTENS

SKILL LEVEL: Experienced ● ● ● ●

FINISHED CIRCUMFERENCE: 7", fits up to 8½"

FINISHED LENGTH: 9¾"

Materials

Gloss Fingering from Knit Picks (70% merino,
30% silk; 50 g; 220 yds)

MC 1 skein in color Robot

CC 1 skein in color Kenai

US size 2 (2.75 mm) set of double-pointed
needles, or size needed to obtain gauge

1 stitch marker

Tapestry needle

Gauge

34 sts and 32 rows = 4" in chart patt in the rnd

Pattern Notes

Charts are on pages 67–69.

Take care to keep floats on wrong side of work at
an even tension.

You may find it helpful to add an additional stitch
marker to separate hand and thumb gusset
stitches.

SPECIAL ABBREVIATIONS

mCCf: Move CC in front.

mCCb: Move CC in back.

≫ *The mittens are worked as mirror images,
creating matching patterns on the back and front.*

Right Mitten

Corrugated rib creates a dense, firm fabric that is also attractive with its columns of color. When working, be careful to ensure the main-color yarn stays at the back of the work at all times, and that the contrasting color is moved back to the wrong side after working each purl stitch. This prevents accidental floats across the right side of the knitting.

CUFF

With MC, CO 60 sts. Divide sts evenly on 4 dpns. PM and join rnd, being careful not to twist.

Corrugated rib: *K1 with MC, mCCf, P1 with CC, mCCb; rep from * to end.

Rep corrugated rib another 23 rnds—24 rnds total.

Next rnd: With MC, knit.

Next rnd: With MC, knit to end, M1—61 sts.

Next rnd: With MC, knit.

HAND

Work hand according to right mitten chart. When thumb gusset is complete, place sts on waste yarn to be worked later. Continue knitting right mitten chart.

When right mitten chart is complete, 20 sts rem. Rearrange sts so that 10 sts for back of hand are on one dpn and 10 sts for palm are on another. Use Kitchener st (page 76) to graft together.

THUMB

When starting thumb, leave approx 8" tail. If you are left with a small hole where the thumb meets the hand after working the thumb, you can use this tail to sew it closed.

Transfer thumb sts from waste yarn onto dpns. PU 1 st where thumb meets hand. This is the first st of the round. Work thumb according to thumb chart—8 sts rem.

Break yarn and thread MC tail on a tapestry needle. Weave needle through rem sts.

Left Mitten

When working colorwork charts, take care not to crowd the stitches on the needles; rather, keep them spread comfortably apart to prevent puckering from too-tight floats. Take particular care when moving from one double-pointed needle to another.

CUFF

With MC, CO 60 sts. PM and join rnd, being careful not to twist.

Corrugated rib: (K1 with MC, mCCf, P1 with CC, mCCb) around.

Rep corrugated rib another 23 rnds—24 rnds total.

Next rnd: With MC, knit.

Next rnd: With MC, M1, knit to end—61 sts.

Next rnd: With MC, knit.

HAND

Work hand according to left mitten chart. When thumb gusset is complete, place sts on waste yarn to be worked later. Continue knitting left mitten chart.

When left mitten chart is complete, 20 sts rem. Rearrange sts so that 10 sts for back of hand are on one dpn and 10 sts for palm are on another. Use Kitchener st to graft together.

THUMB

When starting thumb, leave approx 8" tail. If you are left with a small hole where the thumb meets the hand after working the thumb, you can use this tail to sew it closed.

Transfer thumb sts from waste yarn onto dpns. PU 1 st where thumb meets hand. This is the first st of the round. Work thumb according to thumb chart—8 sts rem.

Break yarn and thread MC tail on a tapestry needle. Weave needle through rem sts.

Finishing

Block mittens to finished measurements given at beg of patt. With tapestry needle, weave in ends.

≫ *A geometric pattern on the thumb allows both yarns to be carried with short, even floats as the thumb gusset is worked.*

Crossing Paths Mittens Thumb

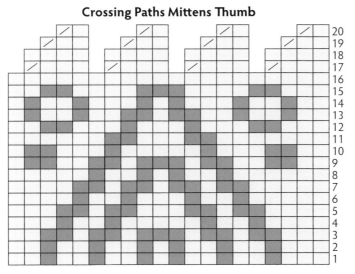

Legend

☐ K with MC

■ K with CC

╱ K2tog with MC

Thumb chart is used for both left and right mittens.

Crossing Paths Left Mitten Chart

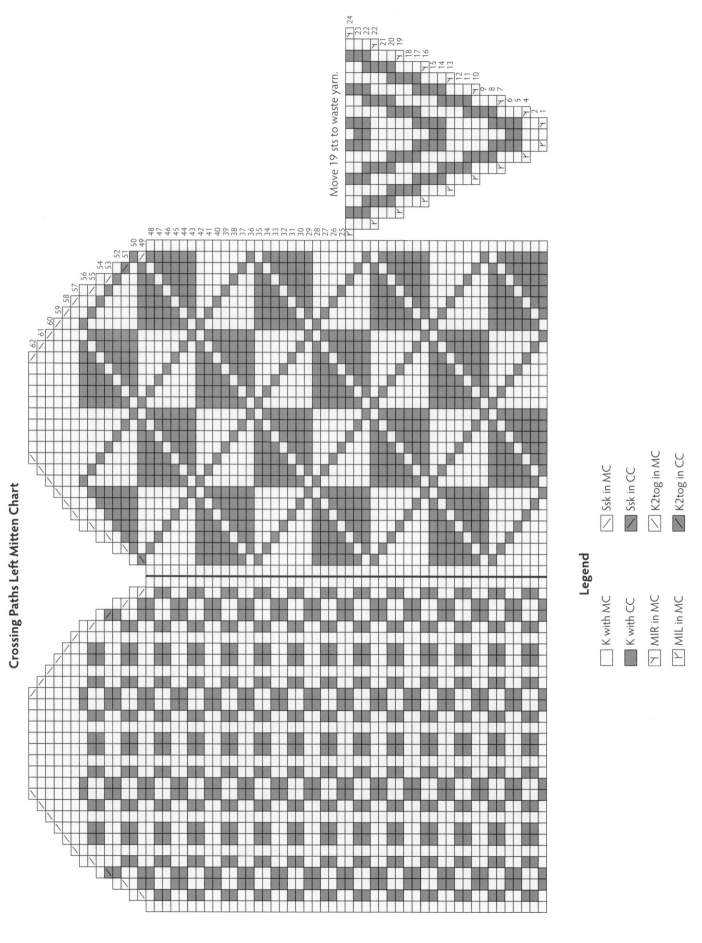

Move 19 sts to waste yarn.

Legend

☐	K with MC	╱	Ssk in MC
▨	K with CC	▨╱	Ssk in CC
⅄	MIR in MC	╱	K2tog in MC
⅄	MIL in MC	▨╱	K2tog in CC

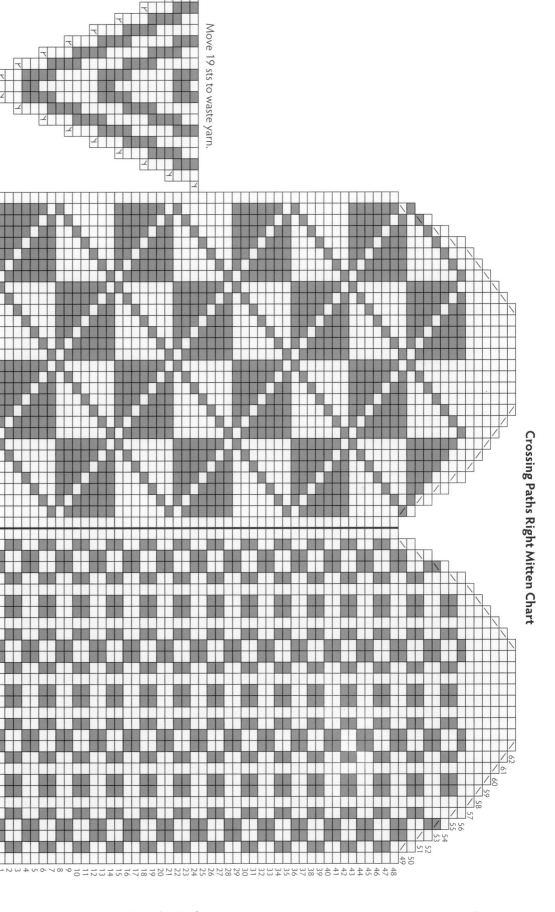

Crossing Paths Right Mitten Chart

Move 19 sts to waste yarn.

Legend

☐ K with MC	◪ Ssk in MC
▦ K with CC	◪ Ssk in CC
◹ MIR in MC	◹ K2tog in MC
◸ MIL in MC	▨ K2tog in CC

Koda

A great cable-and-lace pattern are featured on this scarf and socks set. The purls between the cable panels help give these pieces a ribbed effect—making both the socks and the scarf extra squishy and cozy.

Designed by author and knit by Jenni Lesniak

SCARF

SKILL LEVEL: Intermediate ● ● ● ○
FINISHED MEASUREMENTS: 6" x 72"

Materials

2 skeins of Sock from Malabrigo (100% superwash merino; 100 g; 400 yds) in color Lettuce 🧶 **1**
US size 5 (3.75 mm) knitting needles, or size needed to obtain gauge
Cable needle
Tapestry needle
Blocking wires and/or blocking pins

Gauge

28 sts and 28 rows = 4" in chart patt, slightly stretched

Pattern Notes

Chart is on page 72. If you prefer to follow written instructions for the charted material, see "Written Instructions for Chart" on page 72.

If using a hand-dyed yarn, alternate skeins every two rows. See page 77 for more information.

Special Abbreviation

2/2 RC: Place next 2 sts onto cable needle, hold in back, K2, K2 from cable needle.

Instructions

CO 52 sts. Work chart until scarf measures 72" from CO edge, ending with row 6 or row 14.

> **MAKE IT YOUR OWN!**
>
> *You can adjust the length and width of the scarf very easily. Just add stitches in multiples of 6 (i.e., add 6, 12, 18, etc.) to make the scarf wider. To adjust the length, knit to the desired length, ending with row 6 or 14, before knitting the final row. Remember, changing the size will affect the amount of yarn required!*

Finishing

BO loosely knitwise (page 75). Block scarf to finished measurements given at beg of patt. With tapestry needle, weave in ends.

Written Instructions for Chart

If you prefer to follow row-by-row written instructions rather than a chart, use the instructions below.

Row 1 (RS): K2, *P1, K2, YO, K2tog, P1; rep from * to last 2 sts, K2.

Row 2 and even-numbered rows (WS): K2, *K1, P4, K1; rep from * to last 2 sts, K2.

Row 3: Rep row 1.

Row 5: Rep row 1.

Row 7: K2, *P1, 2/2 RC, P1; rep from * to last 2 sts, K2.

Row 9: K2, *P1, ssk, YO, K2, P1; rep from * to last 2 sts, K2.

Row 11: Rep row 9.

Row 13: Rep row 9.

Row 15: Rep row 7.

Row 16: Rep rnd 2.

Rep rows 1–16 for patt.

Koda Scarf

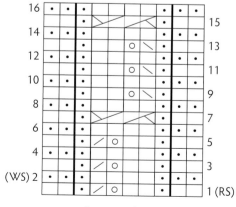

Repeat = 6 sts

Legend

☐ K on RS, P on WS

▪ P on RS, K on WS

○ YO

◥ Ssk

◢ K2tog

2/2 RC

> *The cable and lace give an interesting twist to an otherwise plain ribbed scarf.*

SOCKS

SKILL LEVEL: Intermediate ● ● ● ○

SIZES: Child Medium (Adult Medium, Adult Extra-Large)

FINISHED FOOT CIRCUMFERENCE: Approx 6 (8, 10)"

FINISHED FOOT LENGTH: Approx 8½ (9½, 10½)", or to desired length

Materials

1 (1, 2) skein of Sock from Malabrigo (100% superwash merino; 100 g; 400 yds) in color Lettuce (❶)

US size 2 (2.75 mm) set of double-pointed needles, or size needed to obtain gauge

Cable needle

1 stitch marker

Tapestry needle

Gauge

30 sts and 36 rows = 4" in St st

Pattern Notes

Chart is on page 74. If you prefer to follow written instructions for the charted material, see "Written Instructions for Chart" on page 74.

Special Abbreviation

2/2 RC: Place next 2 sts onto cable needle, hold in back, K2, K2 from cable needle.

Instructions

(Make 2).

CO 48 (60, 72) sts. Divide sts evenly on 4 dpns. PM and join rnd, being careful not to twist.

LEG

Ribbing rnd: P1, *K1, P2; rep from * to last 2 sts, K1, P1.

Rep ribbing rnd another 9 (11, 15) times.

Work rnds 1–16 of chart 2 (3, 3) times.

≫ *There's something so warm and cozy about cabled socks!*

HEEL FLAP

Divide for heel flap as follows: remove marker, heel flap will be worked back and forth in rows over next 24 (30, 36) sts. Rem 24 (30, 36) sts will be held for instep.

Row 1 (RS): (Sl 1, K1) 12 (15, 18) times.

Row 2 (WS): Sl 1, P23 (29, 35).

Rep rows 1 and 2 until heel flap measures 1¾ (2½, 2¾)" or desired length, ending with a WS row.

HEEL TURN

Row 1 (RS): Sl 1, K14 (16, 20), ssk, K1, turn work.

Row 2 (WS): Sl 1, P7 (5, 7), P2tog, P1, turn work.

Row 3: Sl 1, knit to 1 st before gap, ssk to close gap, K1, turn.

Row 4: Sl 1, purl to 1 st before gap, P2tog to close gap, P1, turn.

Rep rows 3 and 4 until all sts have been worked—16 (18, 20) rem.

GUSSET

Set-up rnd: K8 (9, 10), PM to mark new start of rnd. K8 (9, 10) rem heel sts. PU 1 st in each slipped st on side of heel flap. To avoid holes, PU 1 st between heel flap and instep. Work rnd 1 of chart over next 24 (30, 36) instep sts. PU 1 st between heel flap and instep. PU 1 st in each slipped st along opposite side of heel flap. K8 (9, 10) to end.

Rnd 1: Knit to instep sts, work next rnd of chart patt over next 24 (30, 36) instep sts, knit to end.

Rnd 2: Knit to 3 sts before instep sts, K2tog, K1, work next rnd of chart patt over next 24 (30, 36) instep sts, K1, ssk, knit to end.

Rep rnds 1 and 2, working subsequent rnd of chart patt on each rnd until 48 (60, 72) sts rem.

FOOT

Continue working in patt (working chart on instep sts and in St st on sole sts), until foot is 1 (1½, 2)" shorter than desired length, ending with rnd 8 or 16 of chart patt.

TOE

Remove marker, K12 (15, 18) sts to end of sole sts. PM to mark new beg of rnd.

Rnd 1: K1, ssk, knit to last 3 top-of-foot sts, K2tog, K2, ssk, knit to last 3 sts, K2tog, K1— 4 sts dec.

Rnd 2: Knit.

Rep rnds 1 and 2 until 20 (32, 40) sts rem.

Rep rnd 1 only until 12 (16, 16) sts rem.

Finishing

Using Kitchener st (page 76), graft toe. Block socks. With tapestry needle, weave in ends. Block to finished measurements.

Written Instructions for Chart

If you prefer to follow row-by-row written instructions rather than a chart, use the instructions below.

Rnd 1: *P1, 2/2 RC, P1; rep from * to end.

Rnd 2 and all even-numbered rnds: *P1, K4, P1; rep from * to end.

Rnd 3: *P1, K2, YO, K2tog, P1; rep from * to end.

Rnd 5: Rep rnd 3.

Rnd 7: Rep rnd 3.

Rnd 9: Rep rnd 1.

Rnd 11: *P1, ssk, YO, K2, P1; rep from * to end.

Rnd 13: Rep rnd 11.

Rnd 15: Rep rnd 11.

Rnd 16: Rep rnd 2.

Rep rnds 1–16 for patt.

Koda Socks

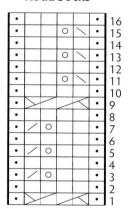

Repeat = 6 sts

Legend

☐ K		◣ Ssk	
⊡ P		◢ K2tog	
⊙ YO		◿◺ 2/2 RC	

Special Techniques

The following techniques are used throughout the book and will help you successfully knit your projects.

Garter Tab Cast On

Several projects in this book begin with a tab cast on. This cast on is typically worked as follows: Cast on three stitches and knit six rows.

Rotate work clockwise 90° and pick up three stitches evenly along the edge. *Try to insert the needle into each of the three bumps on the edge of the tab.*

Rotate work clockwise 90° and pick up three stitches evenly from the cast-on edge (nine stitches total). Turn your work and continue with row 1 of the pattern.

Bind Offs

You can bind off your project in a number of different ways. For a shawl, the goal is to have a bind off that is stretchy so that when you block your shawl you can pull and form the edge any way you like. For other projects like fingerless mitts, you want the bind off to be loose enough to fit over your hand when finished. The following are my favorite knitwise and purlwise bind offs. If you tend to bind off tightly, try using a needle one or two sizes larger.

KNITWISE BIND OFF

When binding off on the right side of the work or following garter stitch, use the knitwise bind off. To work, knit the first two stitches together through the back loop. *Slip the stitch from the right needle to the left needle with the yarn in back and K2tog through the back loops; repeat from * until all stitches are bound off.

PURLWISE BIND OFF

When binding off on the wrong side of the work, use the purlwise bind off. To work, *P2tog, slip stitch from the right needle to the left needle with the yarn in front; repeat from * until all stitches are bound off, ending with P2tog.

Kitchener Stitch

This technique is most often used to close the toe on top-down socks. In this book, it is also used to finish the tops of mittens. It's a great technique to learn—by grafting two pieces of knitted fabric together, you create a seamless piece, which gives your projects an extra-special finished touch. Work Kitchener stitch following these steps:

1. Arrange stitch on two needles, with the same number of stitches on each needle.

2. Thread a tapestry needle with the working yarn attached to the back needle.

3. Insert tapestry needle through the first stitch on the front needle as if to purl and leave on the needle.

4. Insert tapestry needle through the first stitch on the back needle as if to knit and leave on the needle.

5. Insert tapestry needle through the first front stitch as if to knit and slip stitch off the needle.